40 weirdfacts

40 weirdfacts

Written and Illustrated by

CARRIE WEBSTER

Introduction

Here is a weird fact...

This collection of facts has been illustrated with creatures created from fruit and vegetables. No fruit or vegetables were harmed in the making of this book.

Carrie Webster is an artist, photographer, children's book author, mum, and IT specialist, and lives in Sydney, Australia. She spends hours at her computer using Photoshop to transform fruit and vegetables into magical characters set in whimsical photographic landscapes. Carrie is also slightly obsessed with creating monsters.

The Animal Kingdom

The **Animal Kingdom** is filled with **incredible** creatures, large and small.

In this book you will discover some **strange** and **VERY weird facts** about these creatures that will knock your socks off!

From the **enormous komodo dragon** to a **tiny flea**, you will be amazed and astonished at **true stories** of **raining fish**, **dancing skunks** and **freaky goats**.

Plus, see if you can name some of the **vegetables** used to create the **illustrations** throughout the book.

The Animal Kingdom

Stealthy seahorses

Did you know that a seahorse is really a fish?

Not only that, it's the slowest fish in the ocean, moving at a speed of only 1.5 metres (5 feet) every hour. That's slightly faster than a snail. And in case you were wondering, seahorses are NOT related to horses.

A seahorse gradually sneaks up on its prey without creating a disturbance in the water. They can even camouflage themselves in the seaweed to ambush their dinner.

Around 36 species of seahorse can be found in tropical and temperate coastal waters, so keep a lookout!

Ingredients: Beetroot leaf, carrots, spring onions, rambutans, and lychees.

It's raining fish!

It actually rains fish at least once a year at Yoro, a farming town in Central America.

In the Republic of Honduras, scientists say that 'fish rain' occurs when strong whirlwinds develop waterspouts that suck up fish and other marine life from the water. Sort of like a big vacuum cleaner in the sky. The whirlwinds can carry the fish long distances through the air, only to bucket them down with the rain at a different location.

Wait! Does this mean the movie *Sharknado* could be real?

Ingredients: Seed pods, and a surprised farmer.

Unicorns of Scotland

The unicorn is the national animal of Scotland, where people really do celebrate National Unicorn Day on April 9 each year.

While western civilization believed for thousands of years that unicorns were real, sadly, we know today that they are creatures of legend. Belief in unicorns was especially strong in the mid-18th century, as a symbol of purity, innocence, and power.

The Scots associate the unicorn with dominance and bravery, which may be why the first unicorn appeared on the Scottish royal coat of arms way back in the 12th century.

Why didn't they use the Loch Ness monster as their national animal? Oh, that's right: It's a monster.

Ingredients: Sweet potato, spring onions, purple carrots, artichokes, eggplant, and turnips.

Mercedes boxfish car

Is it a fish or a car?

The boxfish is sometimes called a trunkfish or a cowfish, owing to its distinctive box-like shape. In the wild, the species can grow up to 19 inches long, not really long enough for a car.

Yet in 2005, Mercedes-Benz released a concept for a new car that was inspired by the boxfish's unusual shape. They believed the fish-like structure would improve the aerodynamics and stability of the car. They even referred to the vehicle as 'Bionic'.

Sadly, it was never released. And later research showed the aerodynamic qualities of the boxfish were poor compared with most other body shapes of fish. In fact, the boxfish shape actually promotes instability.

Well Mercedes, that was a fishy idea gone square-shaped!

Ingredients: Lemons, celeriac, and avocados.

Wise old owls

But what would you call a group of them?

Everyone knows that owls are considered knowledgeable and wise, which might be why a group of these remarkable birds is called a 'parliament'. A parliament also refers to a legislative body of government, or more simply, a group of politicians. Given owls are mostly solitary creatures, it is not a common spectacle to see a parliament of owls.

Owls mostly live alone, unless they are mating. And they hunt solo, for reasons of survival. Who wants to share the food you have painstakingly stalked, pursued, and hunted with someone else? HOO?

Ingredients: Artichokes, hazelnuts, spring onions, and figs.

The amazing octopus

They are the smartest of all invertebrates.

Scientists say that octopus have been known to solve puzzles. In captivity, they have been caught on camera climbing from one tank and into another, eating the fish and then returning.

Each of their eight arms (no, they are not called tentacles) have mini brains, and octopus have good long-term memory. And no less than three hearts.

Imagine having multiple brains AND hearts. And all the multi-tasking you could do with eight arms.

Ingredients: Buddha's hand fruit, rambutans and tamarillo.

A singing mouse

The male mouse serenades the female by singing like a bird.

The male mouse attracts a mate by cooing its own 'mouse melody' pitched at ultrasonic frequencies, meaning the sound is so high that it can't be heard by humans. Researchers have therefore now added mice to a very short list of singing mammals, which includes only bats, whales, and human beings (except for most Dads everywhere, who definitely can't sing).

Perhaps we should have a newfound respect for these little rodents, who are also exceptionally clean.

Ingredients: Pears, lychees, rambutans, artichokes, persimmon, turnips, and strawberries.

The jumping flea

Did you know a flea can jump 80 times its own height?

In fact, if a flea were the size of a human, it could jump as high as the Eiffel tower. The illustration here is to scale, so the pencil is actually 80 times taller than the tiny flea on the podium: Yes, the black dot.

Jumping great heights allows a flea to propel itself onto its chosen host (a mammal or bird). And fleas can't fly, although jumping so high is almost as good as flying.

Perhaps this is why people imagine they have magic circuses just for fleas.

Ingredients: Pencil, wooden ladder, podium, and a flea.

THE AMAZING JUMPING FLEA

FLEA CIRCUS

Crazy chameleon

Can you see in two directions at once?

A chameleon can focus on two things separately: one with each eye. This is called 'monocular' vision. It can then switch to 'binocular' vision by focussing both eyes together. This increases the chameleon's accuracy as it quickly shoots out it's sticky tongue to capture some lunch.

Imagine being at the dinner table with a chameleon and reaching for a chocolate cookie, only to be beaten by a long, gooey tongue!

Ingredients: Lychees, asparagus, figs, bitter lemon fruit, and sin qua (Asian vegetable).

Hot air ballooners

A rooster, a duck, and a sheep were the first passengers in a hot air balloon.

Strange but true. Built by the Montgolfier brothers in 1783, the balloon was launched in Paris as a demonstration for the King of France. Ten minutes later the balloon came crashing down, but the farm animals all survived and were hailed as heroes of the air!

In the re-enactment pictured, Angry Duck is still angry, which is perhaps where all the hot air comes from?

Ingredients: Artichokes, capsicum, turnips, spring onion, pears, persimmon, cauliflower, and sweet potatoes.

Loads of ants

It is estimated that the total weight of all ants is equal to the total weight of all humans.

Although this is difficult to prove or disprove. Because who is going to weigh all the ants AND all the humans, or even just one or the other? Still, it's a pretty mind-blowing possibility.

Ants are believed to outnumber humans about a million to one. Um, that's one million ants for every human. So, where are they all?

The ant species have been around for at least 30 million years; a long time compared to humans, who have only roamed Earth for a measly 200,000 years.

Ingredients: Purple carrots, persimmon, tamarillo, and rambutan.

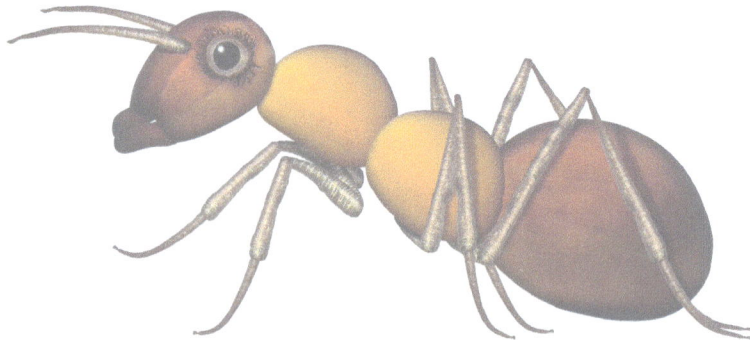

The star-nosed mole

This mole's nose has 22 tendrils to sniff out its favourite food.

It would be like having two and a bit hands coming out of each nostril! Each tendril is like a finger, constantly moving and five times more sensitive than human fingers.

In only eight milliseconds, this mole's nose can decide whether something is edible or not. This is one of the fastest responses to a stimulus in the entire animal kingdom. They obviously haven't compared the star-nosed mole to kids eating cake at a birthday party.

These moles are also able to smell underwater, by exhaling air bubbles onto an object, and then inhaling the bubbles to carry the scent back up through its nose.

Ingredients: Kiwi fruit, turnips, rambutans, fig, and pineapple.

Snails have teeth?

The common garden snail has over 14,000 of them.

Who would think these benign little molluscs could have so many? Some species have more than 20,000 teeth. Better be extra careful in your veggie patch!

Here are some snail facts to chew on. Snail-like animals that do not have a shell are usually called slugs. Some snail species can live for 25 years. The term 'a snail's pace' is used to describe something that is very slow.

Ingredients: Real snail shell, pumpkins, beans, sweet potatoes, turnips, and squash.

Sad little pig

Pigs can't look up.

The only way pigs can see above themselves is to lie on their backs, or to look in a reflective puddle of water. Pigs don't have the muscles in their neck to allow them to move their heads up.

Those nasty green guava birds love to taunt little orange piglet mercilessly every day, just because he can't look up to see them flying above him. Poor piglet!

Ingredients: Orange, zucchini, carrots, guava, pumpkin, beans, and brazil nuts.

Moles dig holes

A mole can dig a dirt tunnel over 90 metres (300 feet) long in just one night.

This works out to be around twelve metres an hour, which is the same as the height of a five-story building. Considering they can be less than twelve centimetres long — which is smaller than the size of an adult hand — moles are incredibly fast diggers.

Moles spend most of their life underground. They have claws built for digging and tiny eyes, which protect them from dirt and infection. Moles are considered pests in some northern parts of the world.

How can you not fall in love with these amazing little creatures?

Ingredients: Kiwi fruit, turnips, figs, and a purple carrot.

Love rats

A pair of rats can produce nearly half a billion descendants in just three years.

The average lifespan of a rat living in a city is one year. During this time, a male and female rat can produce up to 15,000 descendants. (A descendant means their children and their children's children and so on.)

The reasons our planet is not Planet Rat (at least, not yet) is due to pest control, food shortages, predators, and disease.

That means that by the time a rat turns one, they would be celebrating 1,250 family birthday parties EVERY MONTH! Woo-hoo!

Ingredients: Purple sweet potato, artichoke, persimmon, strawberries, and carrots.

Freaky goat

Some breeds of domestic goats faint when they are scared.

Known as a 'myotonic' breed of goat, its muscles completely freeze for about ten seconds if it becomes scared. This usually results in the goat falling over on its side.

The extreme reaction is due to a genetic condition that the myotonic goat is born with. Not so good from an evolutionary perspective, as they would be easy prey. But many people find this behaviour amusing and, for this very reason, choose to have them as pets.

Even you might fall over sideways when you see how many YouTube videos there are about these hilarious goats!

Ingredients: Potato, turnips, zucchini, beetroot, and persimmon.

An army of frogs

Forget about flocks, herds and schools - a group of frogs is an 'army'.

Frogs are social creatures that live together in groups. During the mating season, male frogs croak very loudly to attract females. When a female hears a croak that she likes the sound of, the male grabs her and she releases her eggs for him to fertilize.

In fact, a female frog can lay as many as 4000 eggs at one time. Now that's one huge army of babies to feed!

Ingredients: Pumpkins and persimmon.

Demon duck of doom

Australian, prehistoric, and flightless. Probably ate horses.

The *bullockornis planei*, or 'Demon duck of doom' was one enormous bird with an immensely powerful and sharp bill. It belongs to a family of now extinct flightless birds.

The Demon duck stood around 2.5 metres (8 feet) tall and weighed around 300 kilograms (660 pounds). Not a bird you want to make angry!

Believed to have lived in the Northern Territory of Australia, these birds may have first appeared around 26 million years ago and lived happily until their extinction around 50,000 years ago.

Ingredients: Pears, artichoke, turnips, sweet potato, carrots, spring onions, and tangelo.

Dance of the skunk

The spotted skunk performs handstands as a way of appearing bigger whenever it feels threatened.

Even though the animal is most famous for its smelly spray oil, it can take up to a week to replenish supplies after delivering a squirt. Until then the handstand dance is a skunk's first line of defence. Skunk spray has been compared to tear gas, as it can irritate your eyes and nose, causing redness and tears.

If you are ever lucky enough to see a spotted skunk in handstand action, take it as a warning: RUN!

Better to safely watch them on YouTube instead.

Ingredients: Pineapple, eggplant, turnips, and a fig.

The poison dart frog

One spike of poison from this toxic frog can kill ten grown men.

Poison dart frogs (members of the *Dendrobatidae* family) come in the most beautiful colours and patterns you will ever see in nature: Yellow, gold, copper, green, blue, black, and of course, strawberry red.

In the wild, they are one of the most toxic animals on Earth, thought to be due to the insects they eat. When raised in captivity, however, these frogs are not poisonous at all.

Eating one is still NOT recommended, no matter how much you love strawberries!

Ingredients: Strawberries and red capsicum.

The astonishing dragonfly

After five years as an aquatic nymph, it may only live for a few weeks after leaving the water.

Think 'stealth fighter jet' when it comes to a dragonfly's flying ability. Speed, distance, and flexibility while hunting makes a dragonfly one of the most exceptional fliers on the planet. Their flying ability is so extraordinary that it has inspired engineers to design robots that emulate the flight of a dragonfly.

Having evolved over 300 million years to be the first winged insect on the planet, surely the dragonfly could survive for a bit longer after finally flying!

Ingredients: Beetroot leaves, limes, purple carrots, pomegranate, bitter lemon vegetable, and an artichoke.

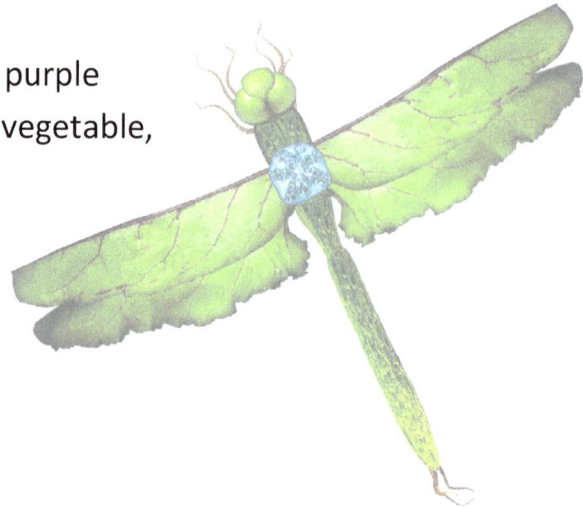

An iguana has three eyes

There is an extra one on top of its head to perceive brightness and movement.

It's called the 'parietal' eye and helps the iguana to evade predators.

Research shows the third eye helps these reptiles see days and nights becoming longer or shorter, which tells their brain when the seasons are changing. In turn, this helps them monitor sleep and reproduction cycles.

Many mums have a third eye in the back of their head, at least, that's what some kids believe to be true ...

Ingredients: Seed pod, limes, beans, and a fig.

Pea-brain ostrich

The ostrich has the largest eyes in the animal kingdom, which, sadly, are bigger than its brain.

The flightless ostrich is the world's largest bird. And the fastest runner of any two-legged bird or animal. It can sprint at over 70 kilometres (43 miles) per hour, covering up to five metres (16 feet) in a single stride. Despite this, the ostrich struggles to evade predators, mainly because it tends to run in circles. Silly bird-brained bird!

Even so, an ostrich can be territorial and aggressive, as well as pea-brained. If feeling threatened, it may use its powerful legs and beak to lash out. Never try and reason with an angry ostrich, just back away slowly.

Ingredients: Rambutans, lychees, blueberry eyes, and of course, a pea.

Incredible komodo dragon

The largest living lizard just grows and grows and grows...

A komodo dragon is an indeterminate grower, meaning it never stops growing in length or weight for as long as it lives. The largest verified specimen of a komodo dragon reached a length of 10.3 feet (3.13 meters) and weighed 366 pounds (166 kilograms).

Komodo dragons are carnivores, or meat-eaters, and also cannibals, which means they eat other komodo dragons. In fact, newly hatched dragons run to climb the nearest tree to avoid being eaten by an adult komodo dragon. What a stressful introduction into the world! Despite such scary beginnings, they are thought to live for up to 30 years in the wild.

Ingredients: Avocados and sweet potato.

The Human Condition

If you think that **animal facts** are weird, wait until you see the **bizarre** and **peculiar** behaviours of **humans**. From **fear of ducks** to an **uncontrollable hand** that **wakes you up** in the middle of the night, these next facts explore some of the more perplexing conditions that make **humans so unique**.

And **WEIRD**.

The Human Condition

Alien hand syndrome

What happens when one hand has a mind of its own?

Alien hand syndrome is a rare neurological condition that usually affects the left hand. Sufferers have reportedly needed to stop their own hand from hitting, punching, or strangling them. One man recounted that his hand would sometimes wake him up at night by hitting him on the head. It sounds hilarious, but also horrible. And it would be really annoying, especially if you were in the middle of a good dream!

Luckily, there have only been around 40 cases diagnosed, ever.

Ingredients: Feijoa, grapes, artichoke, beans, sweet potato, and Buddha's hand fruit.

Orange skin?

Eating too many carrots might prompt your friends to ask: 'Hey, love your fake tan. It's orange.'

If you ate three very large carrots each day for a few weeks, your skin may actually turn orange. This discoloration is a rare condition called *carotenemia* and is most noticeable on the palms of your hands and the soles of your feet. It is caused by a substance in carrots called 'beta-carotene'. Other foods with beta-carotene in them include apricots, cantaloupe, mangoes, oranges, and pumpkin.

Can you see the likeness of this orange man with a certain US ex-politician?

Ingredients: Carrots, mandarins, spring onions, pear, turnips, hazelnuts.

Sweet dreams

During some stages of sleep, your body becomes paralysed to stop you acting out your dreams.

Can you imagine falling out of bed every night because you were moving around in your dream? Thankfully, sleep paralysis is the mind's way of protecting you from doing something physically dangerous to yourself while you are dreaming.

Sleep paralysis can also occur for a short period of time when you are waking up and unable to move. This can be very disorientating, especially when half-asleep and your dream is still going!

Ingredients: Banksia, peppers, carrots, pears, figs, hazelnuts, oranges, celeriac, and plums.

So many bugs!

It is estimated that an adult human may contain up to four kilograms of bacteria, or 'bugs'.

It's not really something we like to think about. But medical research on gut microbes indicates that rather than being small and creepy, bugs are actually far more beneficial for us than once thought. Gut microbes are made up of bacteria and other microorganisms found in our intestines. They help with digestion, metabolism, immunity, and brain functions.

Four kilograms of germs inside your body? Ew! Just can't stop thinking about this now.

Ingredients: Cucumbers, figs, carrots, and rambutans.

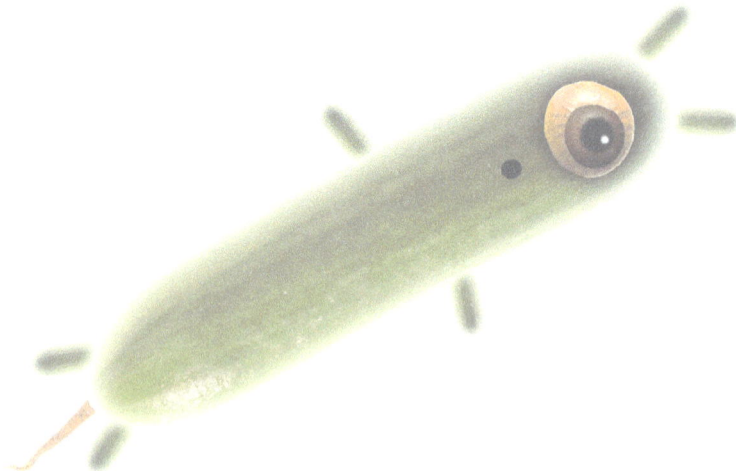

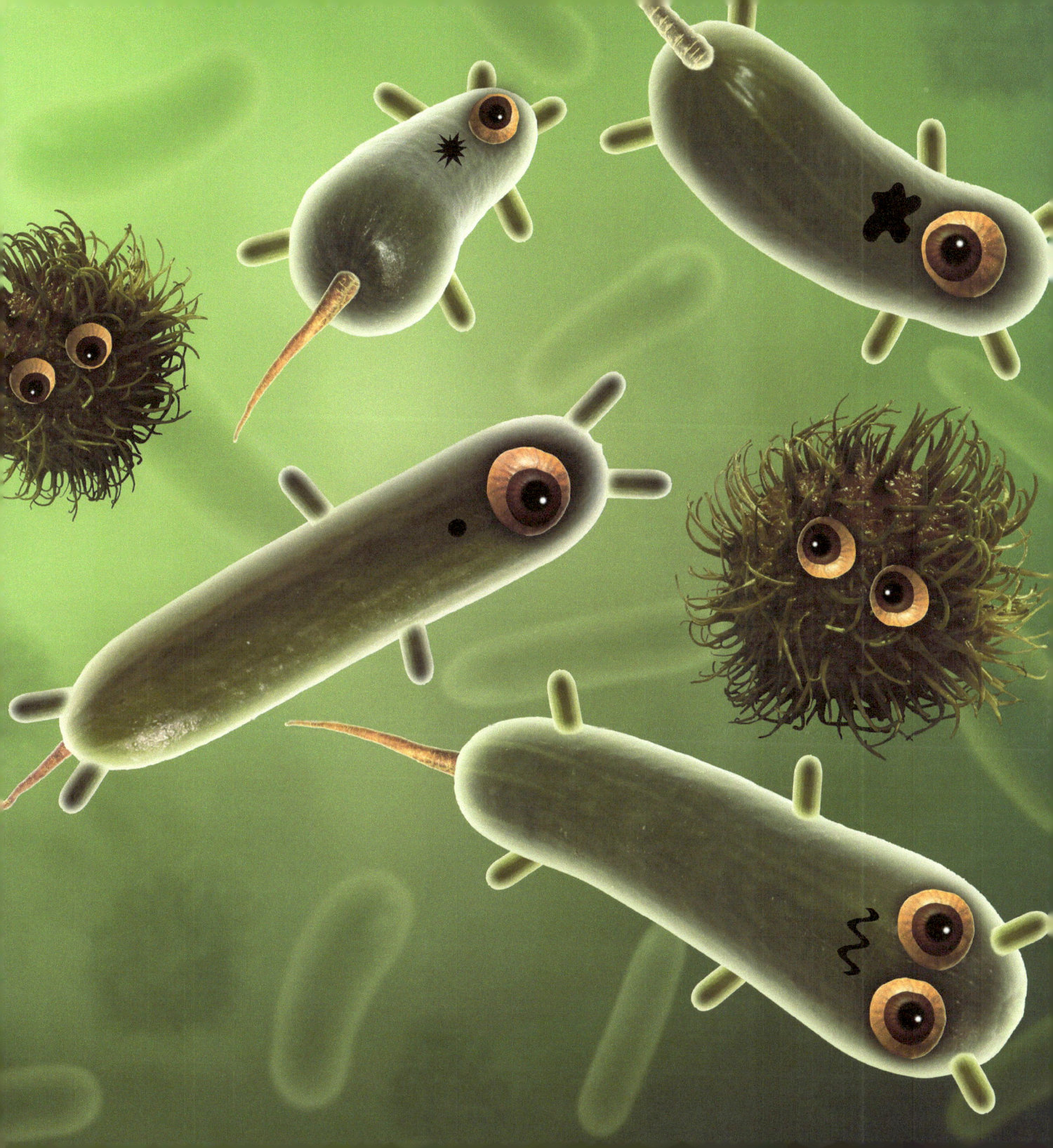

Udderly unbelievable!

Boanthropy is a documented psychological disorder... where a person believes they are a cow.

This very uncommon disorder was first documented in the Bible but has also been recorded in more recent times when a person is in a delusional state. They attempt to behave and live as a cow.

If you have any of these symptoms, seek medical help urgently:

- Walking like a cow on all fours.
- Mooing instead of speaking.
- A craving for grass and hay.

Walking past a paddock recently, this scene came to mind ...

Ingredients: Melon, zucchini, potatoes, basil, blueberries, beetroot, and asparagus.

Aliens amongst us

In 2010, a survey showed that one in five people across 22 countries believe aliens walk among us.

And they are disguised as humans. The poll of 23,000 people by Reuters Ipsos revealed the countries with citizens most likely to believe that there were alien visitors disguised as humans walking or living among them were India (45%) and China (42%).

What a crazy idea for a survey!

Aliens might exist. But perhaps there are more people disguised as aliens than the other way around. What do you think?

Ingredients: Guava, beans, grapes, buddha's hand fruit, turnips, choko, and spring onions.

Fear of ducks

Anatidaephobia is the fear of being watched... by a duck.

A phobia is an extreme and irrational fear of something. Being scared of a duck at your local pond that bit you is rational. Being terrified of all ducks everywhere in the world because you believe that one is watching you right at this very moment, is not rational.

People with *anatidaephobia* cannot stop feeling this intense fear, even when just thinking about a duck. It sounds amusing, but it is very real to those who suffer from this phobia.

No ducks were hurt or made angry in the making of this artwork (although some pears were photographed without their consent).

Ingredients: Pears, artichokes, carrots, persimmon, and a scared man.

The dancing disease

In 1518, an unusual condition saw hundreds of people dance themselves to death.

The dancing plague was a case of dancing mania that occurred in the Holy Roman Empire in the year of 1518. Around 400 people took to dancing for days without rest. During a period of one month, some people collapsed and even died of heart attack, stroke, or exhaustion.

Theories about the cause of the dance mania include stress-induced mass hysteria, or people accidentally ingesting ergot, which is a toxic mold from damp rye that can create hallucinations.

In this re-enactment, the western shirt, jeans, and boot scooters were worn mainly for their ridiculous appearance. What is your favourite? The frock, or the daggy dance moves?

Ingredients: Crazy dancing men.

Can You See Your Nose?

Yes, you always can, though your mind chooses to ignore it.

Luckily for us, there is a very good reason our brains choose to ignore our nose, which is always in our field of vision. The brain does so through a process called 'unconscious selective attention', which allows us to use our brains more efficiently by not registering things that are not so important.

If the nose is not useful information, our brain decides we don't need to see it. Given we can only focus on one thing at a time, it makes sense to filter out visual objects that will distract us.

Fortunately for this monster, he doesn't notice his nose. If he did, he probably wouldn't notice anything BUT his nose.

Ingredients: Pears, watermelon, beetroot, hazelnuts, sweet potato, tomato, turnips, purple carrots, and persimmon.

Fancy a very long stroll?

In the average person's life of 80 years, they will take enough steps to have walked around the earth five times!

The average active person takes around 7,500 steps each day. By the age of 80 years, they will have walked approximately 110,000 miles (177,000 km), which is the equivalent of walking five times around the earth right on the equator.

Why hasn't anyone included monster steps in this calculation?

Ingredients: Watermelon, beetroot, pears, pineapple, coconuts, artichokes, spring onions, hazelnuts, turnips, zucchini, carrots, persimmon, cucumbers, and celeriac.

Trembling at the knees

Genuphobia is an irrational fear of knees; your own, or even someone else's knees.

Genuphobia (from Latin word *genu* meaning 'knee') is a rare phobia that can be caused by witnessing or experiencing a traumatic knee injury. Alternatively, it might also be caused if you come from a highly conservative religious background where knees are always covered. Some sufferers experience extreme anxiety just thinking about knees, let alone seeing them.

Ingredients: Celeriac, watermelon, turnips, sweet potatoes, bitter lemon fruit, and a seed pod.

Other Weird Stuff

And finally, these other **weird facts** look at our **earth** and other **planets** from a **bigger perspective**. They help us to realise how **small we are** in comparison to the vastness of our world. And also how **big we are** in comparison to **microscopic viruses**.

Prepare to be **amazed**!

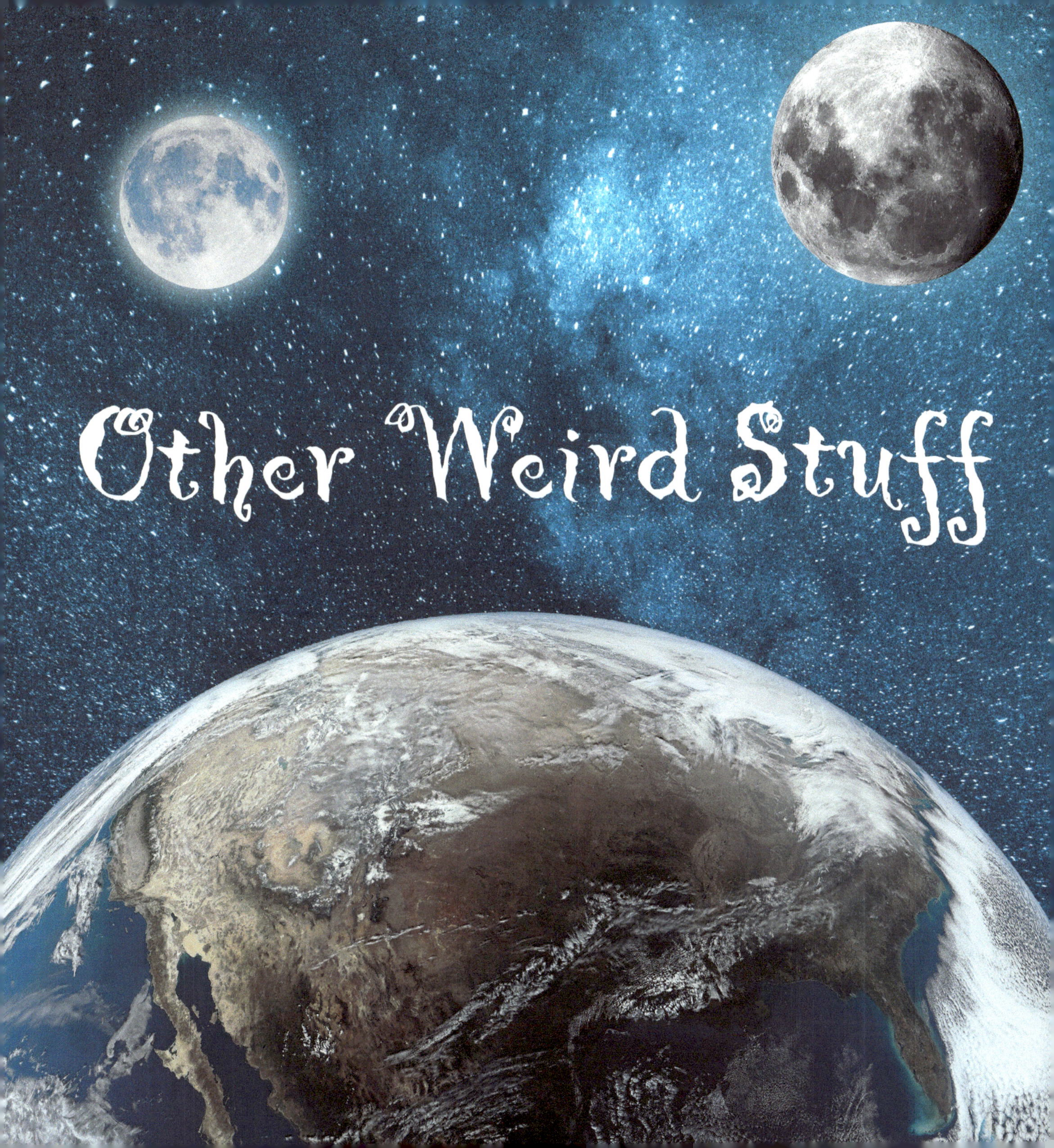
Other Weird Stuff

Blue sunsets

The red planet Mars has blue sunsets.

To the human eye, a sunset on Mars would appear bluish if we were to be watching it from the surface of the famously red planet. Fine dust makes the blue near the sun appear more noticeable, while in normal daylight the red rusty colour is more pronounced.

A Martian friend sent in this photo (Actually, Martians probably aren't real, but it's a good story!)

Ingredients: Pumpkin, artichokes, limes, beans, buddha's hand fruit, and grapes.

Speaking of moons...

Earth may once have had two of them.

The two moons may have collided, which explains why the opposite sides of the moon are so different. This would have occurred billions of years ago.

Scientists suggest this second, much smaller moon, crashed in slow motion into the larger moon. It formed an extra thick layer of solid crust rather than a crater, ending up sort of like a pancake squashed by gravity on one side.

It must have been around the time when orange monsters roamed freely on the planet, but that could be wrong.

Ingredients: Oranges, turnips, persimmon, hazelnuts, and asparagus.

Water everywhere...

Did you know that oceans cover 70% of our planet?

And only 20% of our oceans are visible to us at the surface. So, the 80% of the oceans that lie below the surface, remain unexplored and unmapped by humans.

Not only that, but an estimated 94% of species that are alive today, live in the ocean. Mere land animals, such as humans, are definitely in the minority. Humans make up only 6% of creatures on dry land. Some scientists estimate there could be as many as a few million species still undiscovered in the oceans.

How many undiscovered sea monsters might there be?

Ingredients: Seed pods, durian fruit, turnips, lychees, rambutans, beetroot leaf, lime, Buddha's hand fruit.

Want to host a virus?

There are more of them on earth than stars in the universe.

It is estimated there are 10 nonillion (that's 10x10x10 up to 31 times) individual viruses on the planet, which is 100 million times more than the number of stars.

Trouble is, most viruses can only replicate with the aid of a host, that is, a place to live, like in a living organism such as bacteria, plants, animals, and even humans. Luckily for us, the virus pathogens are very picky about the cells they infect, so only an infinitesimally small fraction of the viruses that exist pose any threat to humans.

Such a relief! We are having enough trouble dealing with the ones we have now, thanks.

Ingredients: Rambutans and lychees.

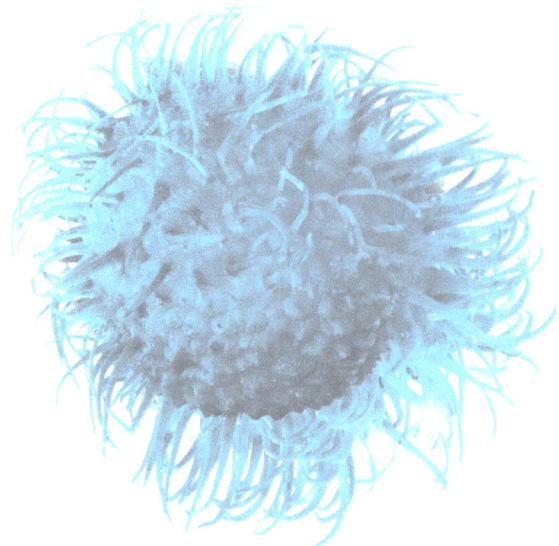

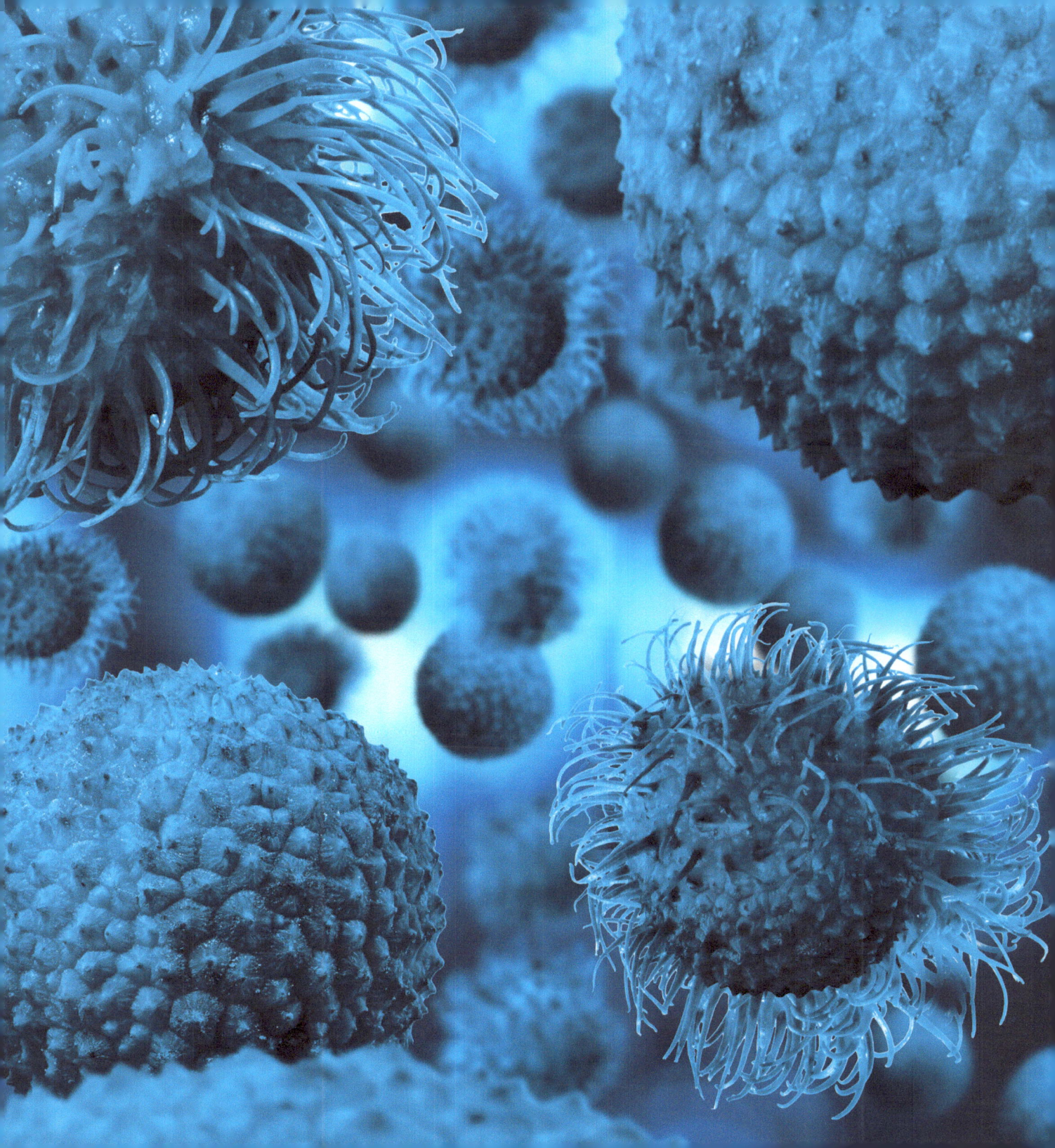

The End

Only of this book. Not the world.

If you loved reading about all these weird facts, it would be amazing if you could please leave a review at Amazon.

Just search for "40 Weird Facts" to leave a review.

You can view my other artwork and order prints here:

www.carriewebster.com